Flute Student

by Fred Weber in collaboration with Dougla ensland

To The Student

This book, with the aid of a good teacher, is designed to help you become an excellent player on your instrument in a most enjoyable manner. It will take a reasonable amount of work and CAREFUL practice on your part. If you do this, learning to play should be a valuable and pleasant experience.

To The Teacher

The Belwin "Student Instrumental Course" is the first and only complete course for individual instruction of all band instruments. Like instruments may be taught in classes. Cornets, trombones, baritones, and basses may be taught together. The course is designed to give the student a sound musical background and at the same time provide for the highest degree of interest and motivation. The entire course is correlated to the band oriented sequence.

To make the course both authoritative and practical, most books are co-authored by a national authority of each instrument in collaboration with Fred Weber, perhaps the most widely-known and accepted authority at the student level.

The Belwin "Student Instrumental Course" has three levels: elementary, intermediate, and advanced intermediate. Each level consists of a method and three correlating supplementary books. In addition, a duet book is available for Flute, Bb Clarinet, Eb Alto Sax, Bb Cornet and Trombone. The chart below shows the correlating books available with each part.

The Belwin "STUDENT INSTRUMENTAL COURSE" - A course for individual and class instruction of LIKE instruments, at three levels, for all band instruments.

EACH BOOK IS COMPLETE IN ITSELF BUT ALL BOOKS ARE CORRELATED WITH EACH OTHER

METHOD

"The Flute Student"

For individual

or

Flute class instruction.

ALTHOUGH EACH BOOK CAN BE USED SEPARATELY, IDEALLY, ALL SUPPLEMENTARY BOOKS SHOULD BE USED AS COMPANION BOOKS WITH THE METHOD

STUDIES AND MELODIOUS ETUDES	TUNES FOR TECHNIC	THE FLUTE SOLOIST	DUETS FOR STUDENTS
Supplementary scales, warm-up and technical drills, musicianship studies and melody-like studies.	Technical type melodies, variations, and "famous passages" from musical literature — for the development of technical dexterity.	Interesting and playable graded easy solo arrangements of famous and well-liked melodies. Also contains 2 Duets, and 1 Trio. Easy piano accompaniments.	Easy duet arrangements of familiar melodies for early ensemble experience. Available for: Flute Bb Clarinet Alto Sax Bb Cornet Trombone

Elementary Fingering Chart

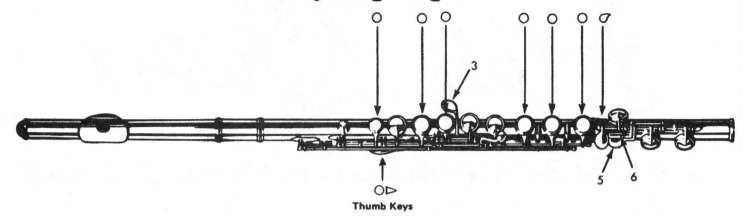

Thumb Keys

How To Read The Chart

● — Indicates hole closed or keys to be pressed.

○ — Indicates hole or key open.

When a number is given, refer to picture of the instrument for additional key to be pressed.

When two ways to finger a note are given, the first way is the one most often used. The second fingering is for use in special situations.

When two notes are given together (F♯ and G♭), they are the same tone and, of course, played the same way.

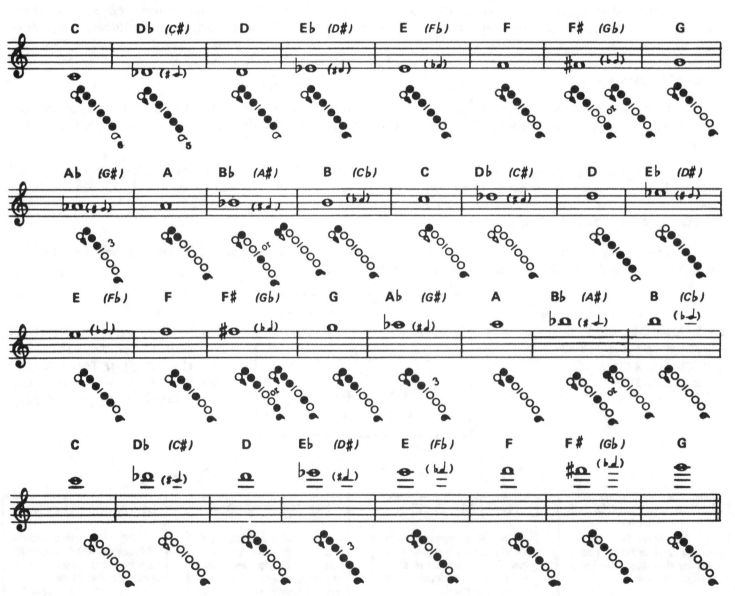

Basic Principles For The Flute Student

EMBOUCHURE AND TONE PRODUCTION

A. Close mouth in gentle, smiling position (not tight), place tip of forefinger vertically against lower lip, and blow over the finger, using the syllable *too* or *dew*.

Use opening about ¼ inch wide and continue this before mirror until sure that lips are directly on top of each other (even profile).

Stretch lips slightly to corners of mouth to eliminate wrinkles.

B. Using only the head joint, place on chin just below lower lip so that about ⅓ of hole is covered by lip.

Do not draw lower lip in against teeth — keep it relaxed and full. Press lips together, firm at corners, relaxed in the center. (Fig. 3)

Use head joint only until both *open* and *closed* tones are clear and on pitch, and can be held 4 or 5 seconds.

1. *Closed* tone (right hand palm covers opening at end) sounds A♭; 2nd space.
2. *Open* tone sounds A♭, octave higher.

POSTURE AND PLAYING POSITION

A. Assemble flute so that both embouchure hole and rod-post of foot joint are in line with center of keys of middle section. Avoid grasp— ing rods when assembling or disassembling flute.

B. Tilt head slightly to right, with flute parallel to lips, and elbows away from body in a natural, relaxed way. (Fig. 1)

C. Left hand — flute against first finger, just above knuckle; wrist bent enough to keep G and G♯ keys under fingers. (Fig. 2)

D. Right hand — thumb under F key or slightly toward E key, flute resting on side of thumb near tip (Fig. 2) (or *tip* of thumb against *side* of flute.)

E. Fingers — slightly curved, with pads of fingers over center of keys. (Fig. 2) Do not permit palm or fingers of right hand to rest on rods.

F. *Always* keep right hand little finger on D♯ key when indicated on chart.

OTHER SUGGESTIONS

1. Use light "tip of tongue" stroke, even on loudest attacks.

2. Tongue starts on ridge just above teeth. Do not stop tone with tongue.

3. Keep lower lip moist and use very little pressure against lip.

4. High tones do not need more air. Hole is smaller and jaw brought forward and upward.

5. Most important position of breath is not that which goes into and across opening, but instead, that which supports the tone.

6. Lower tones require air directed more into opening; for higher tones air is directed more across opening.

7. Blowing over hole too much (with mouthpiece tilted too far outward) results in a windy, harsh tone, sharp in pitch. Blowing down and into hole too much (with mouthpiece tilted too far inward) produces a small, stuffy tone, flat in pitch.

B.I.C.101

24th, take home due.

11, 11th, Studio, recital

Lesson 1   Reading Music

You should know the following rudiments before starting to play:

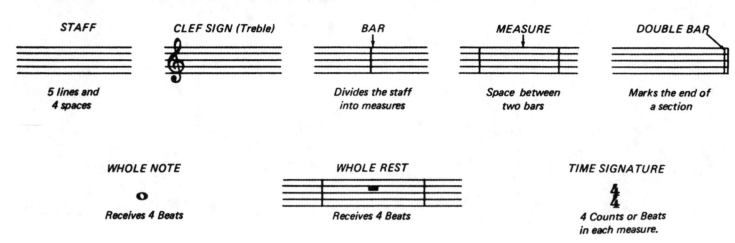

STAFF	CLEF SIGN (Treble)	BAR	MEASURE	DOUBLE BAR
5 lines and 4 spaces		Divides the staff into measures	Space between two bars	Marks the end of a section

WHOLE NOTE	WHOLE REST	TIME SIGNATURE
Receives 4 Beats	Receives 4 Beats	4 Counts or Beats in each measure.

→ Notes and Musical Terms used for the first time are pointed out with ARROWS.
They should be memorized.

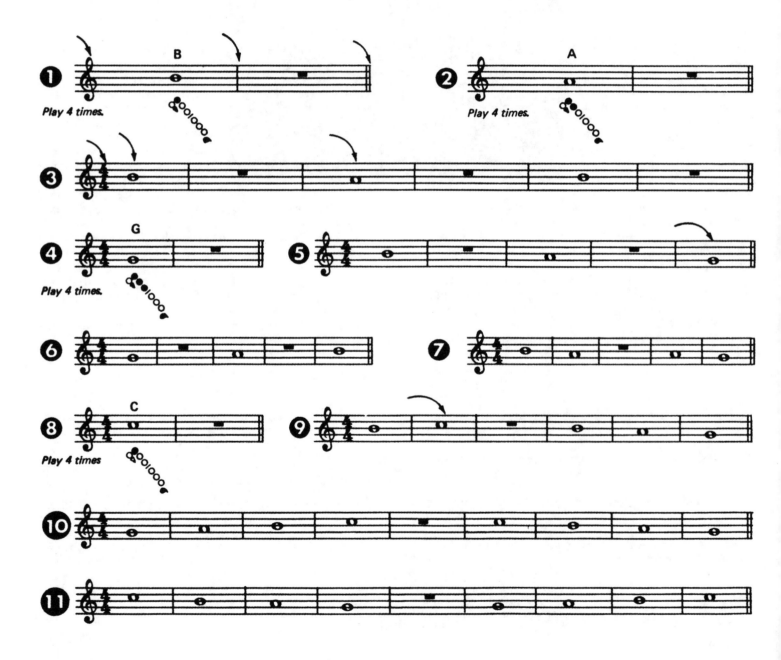

Lesson 2

Quarter Notes And Quarter Rests

Merrily We Roll Along

Famous Tune

PUT THE FOLLOWING ON THE STAFF.

B—Whole Note   A—Quarter Note   A Time Signature   Quarter Rest   Bar   Whole Rest   C—Quarter Note

Lesson 3

Half Notes And Half Rests

Hot Cross Buns

French Melody

The Old Gray Goose

1 Name the notes below. **2** Mark correct fingering.
The First one is done for you.

Lesson 4

Twinkle Twinkle Little Star

Key fingers on proper keys at all times.

Counting Fun

Lightly Row

1 Put notes called for on the staff. Use only notes you have learned. **2** Indicate fingering.

Lesson 5

① ³⁄₄ TIME – 3 Counts in each measure.

REPEAT DOTS
repeat the line.

② (4 Counts)

Count 1 2 3 1

Mary's Little Waltz

③ 1 Play 1st time only.   2 Play 2nd time only.

— 2nd time —

The Cuckoo Waltz

④

⑤ G

Duet

1st Part - (Student)

⑥

2nd Part - (Teacher)

London Bridge (Key of C)

⑦ A

⑧ Octaves - Play slowly.

HOLD – Hold each note as long as comfortable.

⑨

London Bridge (Key of F)

Play 2 times. The first time play entire melody - second time, omit notes marked ★ and substitute a quarter rest.

⑩

By comparing lines 10 and 11 it will be easy to see why we use Key Signatures at the beginning of a piece instead of putting ♯s and ♭s before each note.

* *KEY SIGNATURE* – *means all Bs are played B♭ (See note below)*

⑪

**Sometimes it is necessary to place flats or sharps at the beginning of a line. We call these the Key Signature. This makes it unnecessary to place the flats (or sharp) in front of each note to be flatted. When there is one flat in the signature it is always B♭ and the Key is F. It is in the Key of F because the melody, or study, is based on the scale of F.*

Until No. 11 on this page there has been no Key Signature. When there is no Key Signature the piece is in the Key of C.

Lesson 6

You are now ready to begin the companion books, STUDIES AND MELODIOUS ETUDES and TUNES FOR TECHNIC, correlated with the Method as part of the BELWIN STUDENT INSTRUMENTAL COURSE.

Famous Melody

A-Tiskit A-Taskit

Octaves

Counting Fun

Drink To Me Only

On the staff below, write the note receiving the number of counts called for (in ⁴⁄₄ time).

*When there are two flats in the Key signature, the second flat is always E♭. This means the piece is based on the B♭ Scale and all Bs and Es are flatted.

Lesson 7

SLURS — Tongue the first note of each slur only.   Ask your teacher to explain.

To remind you the note is E♮.

The Old Gray Goose

Repeat line

No Key Signature

Notice

Hold as long as comfortable.

Octaves

March Trio

Lesson 8

Jingle Bells

This means the line may be played either in **C** or **¢** time. Practice the line in
C time until you can play it well, then play the notes *AT THE SAME SPEED*
but TAP in **¢** time (2beats per measure).

The notes will sound the same, only the TAPPING will be different.

Counting Fun
Write counting under notes, then play.

Duet

Write a **T** below the ties and an **S** below the slurs.

Lesson 9

You are now ready to play solos from THE FLUTE SOLOIST, a book of solos with Piano Accompaniments correlated with the Method as part of the BELWIN STUDENT INSTRUMENTAL COURSE.

①

② Check Key Signatures carefully.

③

④ On D.C. Play only 2nd Ending

Fine

D. C. al Fine

Etude

⑤ Work out carefully, then try for speed.

Counting Fun

⑥ Write counting under notes, then play.

Symphony Theme

⑦

Marines Hymn

⑧

Count 4/4 → 3 4   1 2 3 4
¢ → 2 +   1 + 2 +

repeat

FILL IN FINGERING and name note (B♭ or B♮).

Our First Solo

Summer Nocturne

F. WEBER

Lesson 10

Lesson 11

Grandfather's Clock

This is in the Key of E♭.   *See note Below*

Fine

D.C. al Fine

Caisson Song

in Key of B♭

in Key of C

* When there are three flats, the third flat is always A♭ and the Key is E♭. This means the piece is based on the E♭ Scale and all Bs, Es and As are flatted.

Lesson 12

①

means gradually louder.

Apply to scale.

② Also play slurred.

③ Also play slurred.

④

ACCENT MARK — play with force.

Intervals

⑤

The top notes make a familiar melody — Name it.

SIMILE —(means continue in a similar manner.)

Counting Fun

⑥

What famous tune is this based on?

Hail To Our Team — (March)

⑦

❶ Name the notes.   **❷** Mark fingering.

Lesson 13

① Bb Scale

② Thirds

③ Also play slurred.

④ Practice both octaves.

Eighth Notes

⑤

⑥

Your teacher will show you his favorite way of counting eighth notes.

⑦

If the foot-tapping method of counting is used make sure the foot comes UP (Up beat) in EXACTLY the MIDDLE of the BEAT.

⑧ What Key_____?

Skip To M'Lou

⑨

Bicycle Built For Two

⑩

Write the counting under the measures below.

1 2 3 4

Lesson 14

Scale And Key Review

Lesson 15

Scale

①

Thirds

②

Name the Key _____

③

④

This Old Man

⑤

⑥ F#

March Theme

⑦

Venetian Melody

Rhythm Variation

⑧

In the measures below, is the second note HIGHER; LOWER; or the SAME as the first note? Use H, L, and S.

H ___ ___ ___ ___ ___ ___

19

Lesson 16

_____ is intended to picture a well played tone that doesn't wave and stays on exactly the same pitch.

AVOID tones of the type pictured below.

(a) A "Scooped" attack.

(b) A wavy Tone.

(c) Attack not clean.

(d) A Tone that goes flat.

(e) (1) Accented tongue release
(2) Over-accented attack.

Chromatic Waltz

Etude   Name the Key____.

Counting Fun
Write counting under notes, then play.

What tune is this based on?

When The Saints, Go Marching In

Pick Up Notes

Count 4/4 → 2 3 4 1
Count ¢ → + 2 + 1

B.I.C. 101

20

Lesson 17

means gradually softer.   *simile*   means — continue in a similar manner.

Key of G   * See note.

Name the Key_____ .

Name the Key_____ .

Abide With Me

Play 3 times. The first time play the entire melody. 2nd time - omit all notes marked with② and substitute a rest.
3 rd time - omit all notes marked② and③ and substitute quarter rests.

Melody

RUBINSTEIN

* When we have 1 sharp in the Key Signature it is always F♯ and the Key is G. It means the piece is based on the scale of G and all Fs are sharped.

Lesson 18

Work for a steady tone (as pictured) with no change in pitch.

Apply to scale.

EIGHTH REST

Etude

Eighth Note Fun
Name the Tune.

Because You're You

Lesson 19

Staccato — short or separated

Notes with a dot over or under them (♩) are played Staccato. This means to play them short and light. The notes should be separated with a slight rest between each note depending on the character of the piece.

NEVER stop tone by putting tongue between teeth.

Andante From The Surprise Symphony

HAYDN

Etude — (Name the Key _____)

Work out carefully, then try for speed.

Vilia Song

Not too fast

♭ LEHAR

Lesson 20

① **Accent mark**

NOTICE – both ♩ and ♪ notes are separated.   ♩ is accented;   ♪ is not accented.

②

③ Tongue lightly and play with a short rest between notes.   Do not stop the tone with the tongue.

④ Work out carefully, then try for speed.

To A Wild Rose

Slowly and gently

MAC DOWELL

⑤

Lesson 21

Bb Scale — HOLD – Hold as long as comfortable.

PATTERNS
Apply to scale.

ⓐ ⓑ ⓒ ⓓ

Etude

Merry Widow Waltz

LEHAR

Lesson 22

①

Apply each pattern to entire scale in line 1.

ⓐ ⓑ ⓒ (*See note.) ⓓ

f   *p*   *p*
(loud) (soft)

\+ =   *means legato, very smooth, with no separation; the opposite of staccato.*

②

③ Low Eb

Dotted Quarter Notes

DOTTED QUARTER NOTE

④

The author suggests that you tap **twice** on the dotted quarter notes (♩.). The eighth note (♪) comes midway between the 2nd and 3rd taps.

America

⑤

p — stands for *PIANO* and means play softly.

Etude

⑥

Name this Key _____.

College Song

⑦

Lesson 23

Lesson 24

1 This is in the Key of _____?
The Flat is _____?

Thirds

2

3 Db (c#)

like C#

4 ⓐ ⓑ ⓒ ⓓ

Counting Fun Variation

Billy Boy

5

Review Etude

6

Yankee Doodle Boy

March style

7

𝑓 ← stands for FORTE and means play loudly.

Count 1 + 2 + 1 + 2 +

Lesson 25

Scale Etude (Name the Key_____)

Review Etude

Home On The Range

mp ← stands for *MEZZO PIANO* and means play moderately softly.

Under The Double Eagle March

mf ← stands for *MEZZO FORTE* and means play moderately loud.

Lesson 26

Chromatic Review

Always practice both octaves.

Same as D♭

Articulation Etude

Play in a light, separated, manner.

Alternate B♭- *See note below

Famous Melody

Use this new fingering for B♭ in the above line.

Use the new fingering for B♭ while playing this variation. (Try playing it with the regular B♭ fingering.) Which is easier?

Some notes can be fingered more than one way. We call these additional fingerings, Alternate Fingerings. Sometimes it is easier or necessary to use the alternate fingerings depending on which notes come before and after. We learn to use these alternate fingerings now because they must be used later when we learn to play faster.

B.I.C.101

Lesson 27

Also slur.

Always practice both octaves.

*KEY SIGNATURE — See below ***

3/8 Time

See next line.

3/8 TIME — 3 counts to each measure. ♪ - 1 Count; ♩ - 2 Counts; ♩. - 3 Counts;

The Man On The Flying Trapeze

ff — stands for FORTISSIMO and means play very loud.

When there are four flats in the signature, the new flat is D♭ and the Key is A♭. It means the piece is based on the A♭ Scale and all B's, E's, A's and D's are flatted.

Lesson 28

⁶⁄₈ Time

⁶⁄₈ TIME is played exactly like ³⁄₈ except there are 6 counts in each measure. (♩. = 6 counts).

Count → 1 2 3 4 5 6

Sweet Betsy From Pike

(♪=♩)
Same tempo
Don't stop.

Same tempo

My Wild Irish Rose

Name this Key_____.

pp ← stands for PIANISSIMO and means play very softly.

❶ Name the notes. ❷ Mark fingerings.

Lesson 29

Lesson 30

1 →		– receives	1 Count
2 →		– receive	1 Count
4 →		– receive	1 Count

Sixteeth Notes

Count   1   +   2   +

If the foot-tapping method of counting is used make sure the foot comes UP (Up beat) in EXACTLY the MIDDLE of the BEAT.

First practice slowly, then at faster tempos.

Work out carefully, then try for speed.

Variation On Skip To M'Lou

mf

Song Of The Reaper

R. SCHUMANN

With spirit - (rather fast)

mp   1   2   3   4   5   6

Fine

D. C. al Fine

Lesson 31

William Tell Theme

Allegro (Fast)

ROSSINI

American Patrol

March tempo

MEACHAM

Lesson 32

Review

Moment Musical

SCHUBERT

Won't You Come Home Bill Bailey

---

* *When there are 2 Sharps, the second sharp is always C# and the Key is D. This means the piece is based on the D Scale and all Fs and Cs are sharped. The name of the Key is always the same as the line or space 1 note (½ step) higher than the last sharp in the signature.*

Lesson 33

Chromatic Scale

Review Etude

Trepak

Use alternate Thumb fingering for B♭

TSCHAIKOWSKY

Morris Dance

Edw. GERMAN

Fine

D. C. al Fine

B.I.C.101

Lesson 34

Work out all pieces on this page carefully, then try for speed.

Reuben And Rachel

Alternate Fingering *(Review)*

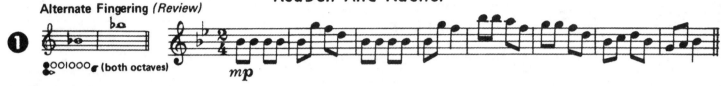

Technical Variation

On this tune use the alternate (thumb) fingering for B♭.

Arkansas Traveler

Variation On Yankee Doodle

The accented notes are a familiar melody. These notes should STAND OUT.

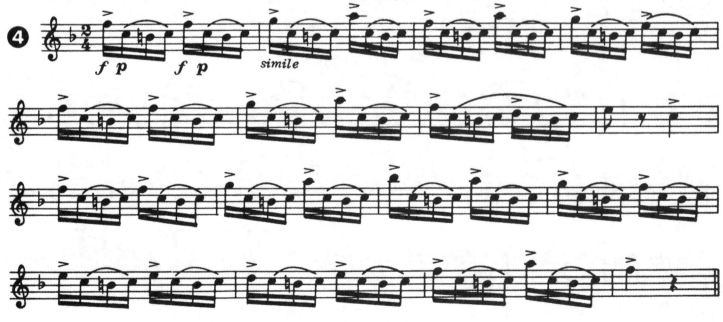

Basic Technic

Scales

Practice all lines with various articulations.

Basic Technic

Practice as assigned by your Teacher

The Patterns below provide for unlimited scale practice in the 7 most common band keys.

FOLLOW THESE INSTRUCTIONS.

Start with ANY line and play through the entire pattern without stopping. Return to the STARTING LINE and play to where the END is marked. You must keep the KEY SIGNATURE of the STARTING LINE THROUGHOUT the entire pattern.

Arpeggios

Eb Chromatic Scale - 2 Octaves

B.I.C.101

40